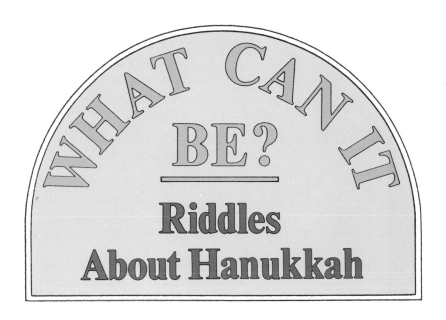

WHAT CAN IT BE?

Riddles About Hanukkah

By Susan Cornell Poskanzer

Photographs by Rob Gray

Silver Press

A Note to Readers: "Hanukkah" may be spelled in several ways: Hanukkah, as you see it throughout the text; Hanukah, or Chanukah.

Published by Silver Press, a division of
Silver Burdett Press, Inc.
Simon & Schuster, Inc.
Prentice Hall Bldg., Englewood Cliffs, NJ 07632.

Printed in the United States of America.

Library of Congress Cataloging-in-Publication Data
Poskanzer, Susan
Riddles about Hanukkah
Susan Poskanzer: photos by Rob Gray.
p.   cm.——(What can it be?)
Summary: A collection of rhyming riddles describing various aspects of Hanukkah and its celebration.
1. Riddles, Juvenile.   2. Hanukkah——Juvenile poetry.
[1. Hanukkah.   2. Riddles.]
I. Poskanzer, Susan.   II. Gray, Rob. 1952–   [1].   III. Title.
IV. Series: Ball, Jacqueline A., What can it be?
PN6371.5.B24   1990   818'.5402——dc20
ISBN 0–671–70553–9 (lib. bdg.)   90–8330
ISBN 0–671–70555–5   CIP   AC

WHAT CAN IT BE? concept created by Jacqueline A. Ball.
For Jacqueline A. Ball Associates, Inc.:
J. A. Ball, President
Ann Hardy, Project Editor
Nancy Norton, Design Consultant

Thanks to: Nancy, Richard, Alexandra, William, Margaret and Catherine Gallin; Danny, Judy, Emily and Max Michaels; Phyllis Gray; Lesley and Niki Achitoff-Gray; Sandy Achitoff; Harvey and Ellen Berenson; West Side Judaica; B'nai Jeshurun; Dreidel courtesy of The Jewish Museum, NYC

A holiday that lasts eight days,
I show up every year.
I come when days are dark and cold,
so many hold me dear.
I bring with me an ancient tale
of courage and of rights.
You may have even heard me called—
the festival of lights.

What am I?

HANUKKAH

Hanukkah is a Jewish holiday that comes in late fall or early winter. It celebrates the Maccabee family's fight for the right to follow their own religion. When they won, they rededicated or pledged their temple as a house of worship to one God. Hanukkah is the Hebrew word for dedication.

A tiny bit of oil
is all that I did hold.
Yet I stayed lit for eight long nights
as it is often told.
I rested in the temple
of heroes brave and true.
I may have done my part . . . and yet
to God, the credit's due.

What am I?

AN OIL LAMP

The ancient temple had an oil lamp that was supposed to stay lit. When the Maccabees returned to the temple, the lamp was not lit. They had only enough oil to burn one day. But a miracle happened: The oil lit a flame for eight days and nights. Today Jewish temples still have a lamp, called the eternal light, that stays lit.

I hold nine candles shining bright.
They sparkle and they glow.
They tell of all the Maccabees
who lived so long ago.
I'm often made of brass or clay.
My meaning's always clear.
I stand for one great miracle
of hopes, and dreams, and cheer.

What am I?

A MENORAH

The menorah of today represents the oil lamp that stayed lit in Judah Maccabee's temple. Today candles are usually used instead of oil because they are cleaner and easier to use.

I help the other candles.
I light them every night.
On Hanukkah I serve the rest
to keep them shining bright.
I'm lit before the others.
You hold me as you pray.
I help you give your thanks to God
for this fine holiday.

What am I?

THE SHAMMASH OR NINTH CANDLE

On the Hanukkah menorah there are nine places. Eight of the places stand for the eight nights oil burned during the first Hanukkah. The ninth place is for the shammash—the candle that is used to light all the others. In Hebrew, shammash means "servant."

We carry your good wishes.
We stay close to your heart.
We let you share your thoughts with God.
At least we help you start.
Before you light a candle,
or right before you dine,
you just may want to say us.
We're words that are divine.

What are we?

PRAYERS

Hanukkah prayers are said holding the lighted
shammash before the candles are lit. The prayers
thank God for the miracle of Hanukkah, for the
Hanukkah lights, and for bringing everyone to the
holiday season.

Sister Jenny,
Brother Frank,
Grandma Sue,
and Uncle Hank.
Great Aunt Sally,
Cousin Pearl,
Nephew Max,
and Grandpa Earl.
We're all the people close to you.
A loving group? Yes, this is!
We come to visit,
bring you gifts,
and give you big, fat kisses.

Who are we?

FAMILY OR RELATIVES

Holidays are wonderful times to get together with family, and share food, news, gifts, and good wishes.

We're crispy.
We're tasty.
We're great fun to eat.
We're always a favorite Hanukkah treat.
We're made of potatoes.
We're fried and we crunch.
So sit down and try us
for dinner or lunch.

What are we?

POTATO PANCAKES OR LATKES

Potato pancakes or latkes are a favorite Hanukkah food in the United States. People often eat them with applesauce or sour cream. In some countries, people prefer doughnuts during the holiday. Both foods are fried in oil. This reminds people of the tiny bit of oil that lasted eight days and nights.

Many tunes we carry
are whistled with great glee.
We sometimes strike a sad chord.
We're sometimes sung off-key.
We share in many festivals.
You really can't go wrong.
So, grab a note that's high or low.
It's fun to sing along!

What are we?

SONGS

Hanukkah songs are often sung at home after the candles have been lit. Some popular Hanukkah songs are *Rock of Ages, I Have a Little Dreidel,* and *Just One Candle.*

You tap your feet.
You feel the beat.
Your heart begins to pump.
You see your toes
skip to and fro.
You make a little jump.
Now form a circle.
All hold hands,
and kick your heels high.
We'll fill your night with lively fun.
Join in and don't be shy!

What are we?

HOLIDAY DANCES

Many people enjoy dancing on Hanukkah to have fun and to celebrate the holiday's great joy. In the most popular, the hora, everyone joins hands to form a circle as they dance around to happy music.

Wrapped in bright paper,
silver and blue,
we show up each night
till the holiday's through.
Bought in a store,
or made by hand,
to get us is great.
To give us is grand.

What are we?

PRESENTS

Many children receive a present on each of the eight nights of Hanukkah. Hanukkah wrapping paper is often silver and blue, and is decorated with dreidels, menorahs, or Stars of David.

Twirl me,
whirl me,
spin me, and then
give me a twist and I'll turn 'round again!
I'm a tornado
that just hates to stop.
They call me a dreidel,
a Hanukkah ＿＿.

What am I?

A DREIDEL OR HANUKKAH TOP

A dreidel is a four-sided top. On Hanukkah, children play dreidel games using raisins, candy, or pennies as counters. The four letters on the dreidel stand for Hebrew words that mean "A great miracle happened there."

We shine like pirates' treasure.
But that's a great disguise.
You'd better look much closer.
You will, if you are wise.
Our middle's made of candy
that's sometimes bittersweet.
We even stop crying children.
And that's no easy feat.
We're coins that you can munch on.
Your taste buds we'll excite.
Pull off our golden wrapper,
and take a chocolate bite.

What are we?

HANUKKAH GELT OR CHOCOLATE COINS

It is an old tradition to give children delicious chocolate Hanukkah gelt for the holiday. Gelt means money. Sometimes children use the gold-covered chocolate coins as counters when they play dreidel.

I'm made of two triangles.
(One's upside down.)
I'm seen on some temples
in many a town.
The symbol of David,
a king and a writer,
I shine with six points,
making Hanukkah brighter.

What am I?

STAR OF DAVID

That Star of David has been the symbol of the Jewish people for thousands of years. It may have first appeared on the shield of David. David was a king of ancient Israel, who wrote many poems and songs.

You buy us or make us.
You send us or take us.
You sign us; then we're on our way.
We make people smile,
whatever our style.
We say, "Have a great holiday!"

What are we?

HOLIDAY CARDS

People all over the world exchange cards through the holiday season to send good wishes, and help family and friends catch up on important news. Hanukkah cards sometimes show a greeting in Hebrew, the language of ancient and modern Israel.

Dreidels,
latkes,
tasty dishes;
songs,
bright candles,
happy wishes.
With all the joys
of Hanukkah,
I stay a good long while.
A grin that spreads across your face,
I'm happy.
I'm a _____.

What am I?

A SMILE

Hanukkah is a favorite holiday of Jewish children all over the world. It is a happy time, shared with family and friends of all religions.